Story Elements

for Middle School Students

Grades 7–8

by
Ann Fisher

Published by Milestone
an imprint of
Frank Schaffer Publications®

Frank Schaffer Publications®

Milestone is an imprint of Frank Schaffer Publications.

Printed in the United States of America. All rights reserved. Limited Reproduction Permission: Permission to duplicate these materials is limited to the person for whom they are purchased. Reproduction for an entire school or school district is unlawful and strictly prohibited. Frank Schaffer Publications is an imprint of School Specialty Publishing. Copyright © 2004 School Specialty Publishing.

Send all inquiries to:
Frank Schaffer Publications
8720 Orion Place
Columbus, Ohio 43240-2111

Story Elemetns for Middle School Students—grades 7-8

ISBN: 0-7696-3400-1

2 3 4 5 6 7 8 9 10 MAZ 11 10 09 08 07

Contents

© Published by Milestone. Copyright protected.
0-7696-3400-1 *Story Elements for Middle School Students*

General Genres

A genre is a type of writing with identifiable characteristics. Some genres you have probably read are biography, poetry, historical fiction, science fiction, realistic fiction, and fantasy. Identifying a story's genre helps you understand its meaning. Read each item below and circle its genre.

1. Amanda thought back to her teenage years, remembering one summer in particular. It was June of 1775. Her family, her village, and her new country were so full of hope. She, too, was full of dreams— dreams of her future as Adam's wife.  They had planned to wed in September, after the crops were harvested and after the younger children in Amanda's charge were back in school. But the Battle of Bunker Hill had changed everything—her hopes, her dreams, her plans, and her life.

fantasy   realistic fiction

historical fiction   science fiction

2. The garper swooped out of the sky and spoke harshly to its owner. "Boy, you must get out of this village! I see a mighty army of trolls approaching from the east. They carry weapons of stone and metal. The villagers here will not be able to protect you. Run, boy, and run hard!"

fantasy   realistic fiction

historical fiction   science fiction

3. Stanley's business was booming! Who would have dreamed that in one summer he could earn enough money to pay for an entire year of college? But that's what was happening. His dad's hardware store was floundering, but its parking lot was huge. And it was right next to the golf course where the biggest golf tournament of the year was going on. Stanley charged $10 per day for every car he could fit into the parking lot, and money was piling up.

fantasy   realistic fiction

historical fiction   science fiction

4. The Jemunites and the Gormonites were engaged in a heavy battle. Weapons were expelled from their transporters at four times the speed of light, bursting into blinding explosions of sound and debris. As a commander aboard the space station in neutral territory, I could only monitor events. How I wished I could stop them!

fantasy   realistic fiction

historical fiction   science fiction

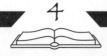

4

Common Traits

Every genre has certain traits. Some genres have some of the same traits. For example, myths and science fiction both tell about events that could not happen. Read the numbered descriptions below. Decide which genres (in the lettered list) possess each trait. Choose the genre(s) that fit each description. Most descriptions fit more than one genre.

Genres

a. biography
b. autobiography

c. historical fiction
d. science fiction

e. realistic fiction
f. how-to manual

Traits

1. tells about events that really happened

   _____

2. tells about events that could have happened

   _____

3. tells about events that probably did not take place

   _____

4. includes facts that can be documented

   _____

5. explains the way something should be done

   _____

6. may include dialogue

   _____

7. may include many technical details

   _____

8. uses make-believe characters

   _____

9. tells the actual story of someone's life

   _____

10. takes place in a believable setting

    _____

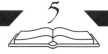

5

0-7696-3400-1 *Story Elements for Middle School Students*

Finishing Fits

Read the scenarios below. Write the names of two possible genres to which each story starter could belong. Choose from the following:

Genres

historical fiction	poetry	biography	mystery
science fiction	folktale	realistic fiction	autobiography

1. Abby drew a deep breath. *How can I ever get out of this mess?* she thought to herself. She had promised her mother she would not play with the slave children unless her parents were home. Now here she was holding a crying baby, with two more little ones tugging at her dress, and her mother was due home any time.

_____

_____

2. Samantha drew a deep breath. *How can I ever get out of this mess?* she thought to herself. Her computerized food manufacturer was flawed. Commanders everywhere had believed her when she told them her new machine could make egg soufflé, chocolate mousse, and baked Alaska. And it could—at least every time she used the machine in the lab. So she had sold a million of the computerized food manufacturers. But here in the café aboard her spaceship, something was different. She just had to find out what it was.

_____

_____

3. I woke up with a sense of uncontrollable excitement. Today I would finally visit the Toledo Art Museum, the place from which five famous Van Gogh paintings had somehow disappeared. The director had told me over the phone that he believed visitors to the museum had stolen the paintings in broad daylight during regular hours, one at a time.

_____

4. I woke up with a sense of uncontrollable excitement. Today I would finally visit Ireland. After we dashed around the house, grabbed a bite to eat, and closed our suitcases for the final time, we headed for the airport. Now I'm sitting in a massive terminal in O'Hare International Airport waiting for instructions to start boarding the plane.

_____

5. This is the story of the cat and the rat.

_____

6. An old man once said, "You're only as good as your word." He spoke from experience as he shared this story.

_____

_____

6

Name _____   Date _____

What Did You Say?

You can learn a lot about a character by reading what he or she says. Read each fragment of dialogue. Then carefully analyze the statements that follow. Write **T** next to the statements that are definitely true. Write **F** next to the statements that are definitely false. Write **E** next to the statements that could be either true or false.

"Brooke, why do you insist on talking louder and longer than anyone else? When will you learn to take turns with the others, to listen when someone is talking, and to remember that you might not always have the right answer?" pleaded Mr. Tull.

_____ **1.** The speaker is a teacher.

_____ **2.** The speaker is frustrated.

_____ **3.** Mr. Tull is in a supervisory position over Brooke.

_____ **4.** Mr. Tull thinks Brooke's behavior is appropriate.

"Ha, ha, ha! Now all of these little lovelies will be thrown into my big kettle and cooked up into a delicious stew. How tasty it will be! Ha, ha, ha!"

_____ **5.** The speaker is going to throw people into the stew.

_____ **6.** The speaker has no idea how the stew will turn out.

_____ **7.** The speaker is a female.

_____ **8.** The speaker is looking forward to eating the stew.

"We need to work together like we never have before. Our work is of utmost importance, and time is running out. More people may die unless we find a workable solution," stated the director.

_____ **9.** The director is dealing with a health problem.

_____ **10.** The director wants everyone to work late.

_____ **11.** The speaker believes the solution will be easy to find.

_____ **12.** It is important that a solution be found quickly.

"The best part of the day is going home to my twins," Gracie told her sister. "How I love to play with them, bathe them, and, yes, I must admit, clean up their many messes. Oh, Amy, how soon, I keep asking myself, will I be able to quit work and stay home with them full time?"

_____ **13.** The speaker is a mother.

_____ **14.** The speaker wants to keep her job away from home.

_____ **15.** The speaker is single.

_____ **16.** Gracie and her sister are close friends.

7

     0-7696-3400-1 *Story Elements for Middle School Students*

Who Says?

Who is most likely to make each of these statements? Circle the letters of all possible answers.

1. "Well, gang, I think we're about finished with this month's big project. You can feel proud of the work you have done. The public will certainly be pleased with the amount of money you have saved them."

   a. a school board president
   b. a pet store owner
   c. a director of a public museum

   d. a construction supervisor
   e. a chair of a governmental agency
   f. a factory worker

2. I chose my profession at an early age. My dad's job was very important, one in which he saved lives and helped a lot of people. But he was never home. I decided when I grew up that I'd pursue a career that allowed me to spend more time with my family.

   a. a firefighter
   b. a doctor
   c. a piano tuner

   d. a writer
   e. a school teacher
   f. a law enforcement officer

3. I welcomed the first signs of spring. Today I saw a robin, cloudless skies, and crocuses poking through the soil. Today I was able to enjoy the fresh emergence of a new season as I strolled through the woods.

   a. a painter of nature
   b. a school custodian
   c. a farmer

   d. a bird watcher
   e. a computer programmer
   f. an electrician

4. This summer means yet another seminar, another workshop, and another thick manual of reports and survey results. If only the world would slow down. Then I could breathe and do over and over the things I already know. But instead, I must keep learning and updating my store of knowledge.

   a. a nurse
   b. a restaurant manager
   c. a hairdresser

   d. a teacher
   e. a computer technician
   f. a landscaper

5. I've lived on this land longer than anyone except Brown. Yes, I was here before any two-legged human or fowl. Brown and I tilled the first acre of this land where he (and later his wife, Sally) planted the vegetable garden. He rode me down the road when he was courting Sally. The little Browns played with me when none of the other animals would let them.

   a. a horse
   b. a hired farm worker
   c. a chicken

   d. a snake
   e. a donkey
   f. a child

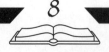

8

Name _____   Date_____

As You Speak

Vivid, true-to-life characters reveal themselves by what they say. Put words in these characters' mouths that reveal something about them. Write two comments that reveal opposite characteristics but are still believable. The first two are done for you.

Angry driver passing a bad wreck on the expressway

1. "Those idiots got what they deserved."

2. "I better get control of myself or I might end up like them."

Yankees losing pitcher after a 0 to 10 loss

3. _____

4. _____

Yankees winning pitcher after a 10 to 0 win

5. _____

6. _____

A girl your age about someone who dislikes her

7. _____

8. _____

A boy your age after a teacher tells him he should work harder

9. _____

10. _____

Your classmate running for student council

11. _____

12. _____

A student meeting a new student for the first time

13. _____

14. _____

9

Name _____   Date _____

The Attic

Read the story and then answer the questions on page 11 about the characters.

"Dad says if we want to go to the amusement park next weekend, we should clean out the attic and have a garage sale to raise some money. So I guess we better get started," said Matt.

"Okay," agreed Molly. "I know we'll have to do it anyway, and it's a good idea to use the money for Cedar Point. I just would rather not be up there in all the dust and cobwebs."

"Whatever," Miranda added.

The siblings opened the trap door and pulled down the folded stairs. Carefully they climbed up, with Matt leading the charge and Miranda reluctantly bringing up the rear. They decided to start with the three sets of bookshelves, with each of them tackling one set.

Five minutes into the task Miranda announced she was finished. "There's nothing on my shelves anyone would want to buy. Old magazines and catalogs and faded Christmas decorations won't bring us enough cash to buy a glass of lemonade. I'm throwing all of this stuff into a garbage bag, and then I'm done," she grumbled.

"Miranda, I wish you wouldn't be so enthusiastic about this," Molly replied sarcastically. "What did you expect we'd find? Besides, we're just getting started."

Matt suggested, "Why don't you open the big trunk that used to belong to Great-Great-Aunt Somebody? Maybe you'll find something cool in there."

As Molly and Matt cleaned their shelves and sorted the knickknacks into piles to sell, save, or throw away, Miranda traipsed over to the trunk. She blew a mound of dust from its top and carefully opened the latch. "Whew!" she whistled. "Life just became a little more interesting. I knew this trunk belonged to a relative who lived a long time ago, but I didn't know that person was famous. Our ancestor was Susie King Taylor. I read her biography last year in school! From this family tree, I'd guess she was our aunt, with about five *greats* in front of that."

"I've never heard of her," said Matt. "What do you know about her?"

As Matt and Molly wound their way through the piles of debris to look at the contents of the trunk, Miranda told them what she remembered from the biography.

"Susie was born a slave in Georgia in the mid-1800s. She was the eldest of nine children, so one of her brothers or sisters must be our great-great-great-great-great grandparent.

"When she was about seven, she went to live with her grandma, Dolly, who arranged reading lessons for Susie. The lessons had to be secret because it was against the law to teach slaves to read. Susie was a teenager when she was freed from slavery, during the Civil War. She taught other freed slaves how to read, and she became the first black nurse in the army.

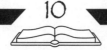

10

     0-7696-3400-1 *Story Elements for Middle School Students*

The Attic cont.

"Her story is in her autobiography, *My Life in Camp*. We can read more about it for ourselves," Miranda concluded.

"That would be terrific! I wonder where we can find a copy of that book," Matt said.

"Right under your nose," answered Molly. "Here's an autographed copy, and it's in mint condition. Who wants to read it first?"

"What? We're going to read it? I thought we'd sell it for a fortune and buy our Cedar Point tickets!" exclaimed Miranda teasingly.

"Oh, no," interrupted Matt. "There's no way we're parting with a family treasure like this. Let's close the trunk and go find more plastic flowers and Christmas wreaths!"

1. Which characters mentioned in the story are not present in the attic?

_____

_____

2. Which character is reluctant to work in the attic?

_____

_____

How do you know? Underline three sentences in the story that show this.

3. Which character seems the most helpful and encouraging?

_____

_____

4. What is Cedar Point?

_____

5. Who wrote *My Life in Camp*?

_____

_____

6. How are Miranda, Matt, and Molly related?

_____

_____

7. Using the story (not a dictionary) as a guide, what do you think the word *traipsed* means?

_____

_____

8. Which character changed the most during the story?

_____

_____

What was the reason for the change?

_____

_____

9. What words in the story give you clues to how the characters were feeling?

_____

_____

10. Choose one character from the story. On another sheet of paper, write a description of how this person might look. Include his or her age, appearance, clothing, and so on. Use the information in the story for clues.

11

Musical Mayhem

When you read or write a story, grids can help you track characters' particular actions and characteristics. Sort out these musical characters for a story about the Medford Middle School Jazz Band. Use the grids to help you sort through the information.

1. Bryce switched from trombone to drums when Justin switched from drums to saxophone.

2. Neither Angela nor Betsy have ever switched instruments.

3. Betsy does not use her mouth when she plays.

4. Vince switched from Justin's second instrument to Bryce's first instrument.

5. Sarah has never played the trumpet or the guitar.

Instruments played first

	Betsy	Justin	Bryce	Angela	Vince	Sarah
drums						
keyboard						
guitar						
sax						
trombone						
trumpet						

Instruments played second

	Betsy	Justin	Bryce	Angela	Vince	Sarah
drums						
keyboard						
guitar						
sax						
trombone						
trumpet						

0-7696-3400-1 *Story Elements for Middle School Students*

Dialogue Details

When reading dialogue, it is very important to keep track of who is speaking and to whom she or he is speaking. Read the dialogue fragments and answer the questions that follow each one.

"Hark, O King! I hear your page approaching. Perhaps he is, at last, bringing news from Yoman in the distant land of Peor. Perhaps we will finally learn if Yoman agrees to help defend us from the Silkonites."

1. Who is being addressed?_____

2. Who is expected to arrive?_____

3. News is expected from whom?_____

4. Who might the speaker be? Choose all that could be correct.

   a. the page   b. the king's military adviser

   c. the queen   d. the leader of the Silkonites

The reporter was persistent. "Mr. President, the American people want to know exactly what you knew about the Vice President's health problems and when you knew it. Did you see Dr. Ryan's report? Did you know she has been quoted in *Current News* as having said that she told you personally there were conditions that might interfere with his performance?"

5. Who is speaking?_____

6. Who is being addressed?_____

7. In the last sentence, the phrase "his performance" refers to whom?

_____

8. The doctor reportedly spoke personally to whom?_____

9. We know the gender of two people in the story. Who are they, and what is each one's gender?_____

_____

10. Whose gender remains unknown?

_____

"Misty, Rudy, Toby, and Zoe! All of you come in right now," Mrs. Miller called. The two children and the two pets came in. While taking a phone call, Mrs. Miller whispered, "We need to leave for Grandma's soon. Rudy, please put Misty out back in the pen with some fresh water. Toby, please change the litter box and make sure Zoe has enough food and water to last overnight."

11. What are Mrs. Miller's children's names?

_____

12. What are the names of the pets?

_____

13. What kind of animals do you think Mrs. Miller owns?_____

14. Choose which words describe how Mrs. Miller might be feeling.

   a. hurried   d. excited

   b. relaxed   e. patient

   c. lazy

Role Play

Director Cam Era is assigning parts for the spring musical. Listen to the comments made by the actors on learning what roles they will play.

a. "This is absolutely fabulous! I get to be spoiled and rich. This should be a blast!"

b. "Why do I always get stuck with playing the part of the idiot? Do I really look or act that stupid?"

c. "What? Only two lines for me in the entire play? How will the audience ever see what a great performer I really am?"

d. "Thank you so much, Mr. Era, for giving me a part in this play. You know this will be my first time on stage, and I appreciate your taking a chance on me."

e. "All I have to say, Rookie, is that you better get it right! The reputation of our entire group is at stake, and we don't need an amateur messing it up."

f. "Yo, Mr. Director. Did you forget about me? If you don't have a part for me, that's okay. Memorizing lines sure takes a lot of work, and it's okay if you passed on me. Like, you know, I could use some free time."

g. "Who has the most lines? Who is in charge of costumes? I heard Evan is doing the choreography. Is that true? What are we having for lunch?"

h. "I…I…I can't believe we're doing this musical. I really hoped it would be *South Pacific*. I want to sing those songs so badly."

i. "Now that all of you have your parts, you should try to spend at least thirty minutes a day learning your lines. When is our first practice, Cam?"

j. "I need to get started on the props right away. They always take longer than you think. Last year I worked twenty hours straight to finish in time for opening night."

Match each quote above to one of the following people. Write the letter of the correct quote next to each number.

_____ **1.** Zachary: bossy, proud

_____ **2.** Devin: frustrated, angry

_____ **3.** Rita: grateful, timid

_____ **4.** Hal: disciplined, serious

_____ **5.** Elaine: nosy, prying

_____ **6.** Phoebe: pleased, excited

_____ **7.** Pete: pressured, worried

_____ **8.** Marvin: conceited, arrogant

_____ **9.** Arnie: unconcerned, lazy

_____ **10.** Gretchen: disappointed, let down

14

Name _____   Date _____

Time and Place

The setting of a story includes the time it occurs and the place it happens. Read each dialogue fragment below. Then match it to the correct time and place from the choices listed. There will be one extra answer in each category.

Times:		Places:	
first day of school	bedtime	concert	gymnasium
lunch hour	a job interview	hospital	deserted island
Christmas	midnight	busy street	school bus stop
soccer practice	sunrise	cafeteria	swimming pool

1. "I never knew how alone I could feel or how dark it could be."

Time _____   **Place** _____

2. "Sorry, guys. I had no idea traffic would be so bad between here and the park. I guess we better eat in the car so we're not late getting back to the office."

Time _____   **Place** _____

3. "Don't worry, sweetheart. It's going to be a good day and a great year. You already know Johnny and Sam. They'll be kind to you. And I packed your very favorite juice in your lunch."

Time _____   **Place** _____

4. "I know you're missing out on a lot of fun while you're stuck here in your room, so I thought I'd stop by and hang out with you a while."

Time _____   **Place** _____

5. "Please demonstrate how to tread water before I make my final decision."

Time _____   **Place** _____

6. "Don't you hate it when it rains on practice days? You can't kick and run in here the same way you can out on the field."

Time _____   **Place** _____

7. "This is the best time of day to be in here. The first light sparkles across the big metal bowls and spotless counters. Everything is quiet, clean, and peaceful. Soon enough it will be loud, sticky, and messy."

Time _____   **Place** _____

0-7696-3400-1 *Story Elements for Middle School Students*

The Storyteller

Read the story and then answer the questions on page 17.

Today the storyteller came to our village. Our yarn spinner travels from village to village telling stories he's heard. He listens to new stories along the way. He comes to our village once during the rainy season and once during the dry season. We await his arrival with great anticipation.

This visit was during the dry season. We looked for cool places to sit, away from the heat of the bright sun, but there was little shade to find. We did our best to sit quietly on the baked earth without fidgeting as the storyteller spoke.

"Children," he began, "today I will tell you the story of how the warthog was named. You see, many, many years ago this land did not have a dry season. Hogs, sheep, leopards, and camels were plentiful. Green crops grew tall. Then, once, the rains came for many days—yes, for nearly three courses of the moon. The great rivers far from here filled to their brinks and flowed over many villages, until they reached this village."

The minstrel continued, "With the river waters came thick, wet earth, such as you children have never seen in your lifetime. In this thick, wet sludge lay the eggs of many unusual creatures. Here, I will show you a picture of one of them."

The children gasped as the storyteller revealed a picture of a frog. They had never seen such a creature. The frog had long jumping legs, a bright green body, and warts!

"Legends say that this creature is known as a frog and comes all the way from ancient Egypt. Long ago, the pharaohs detested frogs and banned them from their country. Where could the frogs go, then, but into the river?

"As I was saying, the mud held the eggs of many, many frogs. The frogs hatched from their eggs and hopped out of the mud into your village. (But remember, this was many, many years ago, long before your great-grandfather was a child.) When this happened, the hogs, sheep, leopards, and camels were a bit upset.

"'This is our village!' the animals cried. 'Frogs do not belong here. We do not want them, just as Egypt does not want them. What shall we do?' they asked one another.

"At last, the animals thought of a plan. 'We shall give the frogs a choice,' they declared. 'Either the frogs return to Egypt or they become one of us.'"

The narrator continued, "Of course the frogs, knowing how much they were hated in Egypt, decided to become one of the animals. But hard as they tried, they still had jumping legs, green bodies, and warts. They could not create the snout of a hog, the fleece of a sheep, the spots of a leopard, or the humps of a camel—no matter how hard they tried. Banishment back to Egypt appeared to be their only option.

"The frog leaders held a grand meeting in which they debated, argued, and cried about their predicament. At last, the frog council offered a plan to the other animals.

16

0-7696-3400-1 *Story Elements for Middle School Students*

The Storyteller cont.

"'Since we cannot become one of you in our bodies, we propose that part of our bodies become part of your bodies. We hereby offer to plant our warts on your hogs and then go in peace to the place where all frogs find their final rest.'

"Solemnly the hogs, the sheep, the leopards, and the camels all agreed, and the deed was done.

"Since that day," the teller of tales concluded, "the hogs of your village have been known as warthogs. The warts from the frogs can no longer be seen on your hogs. Instead, over

these many, many years, the warts became the four large tusks that you see on your warthogs today. And the bright green frogs cleverly turned themselves brown, hid in the bush, and became tree frogs. They continue to live happily among you. If you walk quietly among the trees at night, you may be lucky enough to see one."

With a swish of his robes, the grand fabler swept into the hut of one of the villagers. He refreshed himself with a few swallows of water and walked away toward the next village.

1. On what continent do you think this story takes place?

   _____

2. What phrases in the story give clues to the location?

   _____

3. When did the storytelling happen?

   _____

4. When did the animal fable happen?

   _____

5. Contrast the two settings in the story. Write at least four adjectives in each column to describe the differences.

   a. place where storyteller is speaking

   b. place where fable occurred

   _____   _____
   _____   _____
   _____   _____
   _____   _____

6. Using the context of the story, tell what *predicament* means.

   _____

   _____

7. List all of the synonyms used in the story for *storyteller*.

   _____

   _____

   _____

0-7696-3400-1 *Story Elements for Middle School Students*

The Traveler

I was in for a surprise on January 1, 1995. I woke up that morning (or maybe it was noon) and knew it was the beginning of a new year. I was just eight years old, I'd been allowed to stay up past midnight, and things were looking good. What I didn't know was that 1995 would bring a huge change in my usually predictable life.

Unsuspecting, I yawned and stretched in my comfy flannel pajamas and slid from my warm bed. I went downstairs to the breakfast table (except Mom was already serving lunch). Snow was falling, enough to cover the tracks we'd made yesterday when we built a snow sculpture. A plow, no doubt, would be by soon, scraping fresh mounds to the edges of the straight, flat street out front. The one-hour trips we had taken to the beach last summer were distant memories.

Mom and Dad were intently studying a map I'd never noticed before—a big map of a big island. "Well, sweetie," Dad smiled, "how would you like to move to Ireland?"

You could have knocked me over with a feather (or maybe a shamrock). "You mean the land of leprechauns, potatoes, and fiddles? Cool!" (You see, even at age eight, I was doing a lot of reading, especially about places that seemed more exciting than Indiana.)

And speaking of reading, I remember a lot about school back in Indiana. I rode the big yellow bus that said South Bend Public Schools. Of course, I couldn't read all those words yet, but I knew it was my bus because of the big orange tag in the front window. I especially remember my kindergarten teacher, Mrs. Gibler. She was the calmest person I've ever known. Even when Charlie ran around the room with scissors in his hands, pointing them at everyone, Mrs. Gibler smiled, took the scissors, and (in a very soothing manner), moved us all to the next lesson. Mrs. Gibler was the best. (I see now I have gone down a bunny trail and must get back on track at once!)

Halfway through 1995, we moved to Ireland. As the plane approached the Belfast airport, I was surprised to see thirty-eight shades of green—really! Farmers had divided patches of fields with stone walls, and every patch was a different shade of green. It was surprisingly awesome, even more colorful than I had imagined after reading all the books about Ireland in our neighborhood library.

We settled into a modest home where we had all the amenities: running water (hot, if you remembered to pull the string on the small heater), a flushing toilet (one per house), oil heat (unless you wanted to burn peat in the fireplace), a sturdy stone wall around the house (around every Irish house,

 0-7696-3400-1 *Story Elements for Middle School Students*

which was new to me), and a green patch of "garden" out back. Dad (immediately) and Mom (eventually) learned how to drive a stick shift on the left side of the road and up and down the edges of mountains on narrow, twisting roads.

Neighbors welcomed us with plates of *biscuits* (cookies) and invited us down (at ten o'clock at night) for a spot o' tea. We learned to shop for produce known by different names, to "paddle" (wade) in the salty water at the edge of the Atlantic, to drive to Downpatrick and back, and to begin to feel at home. I learned to endure a winter without snow, although I really missed it. I also learned to endure summer without 90-degree temperatures (which was really no problem).

At first, we homeschooled. That meant lessons around the kitchen table, frequent trips to the tiny library (where we found more Irish and British books than American books), and lunch with Dad (sometimes). Later we moved south and went to the public (Catholic) school, wore uniforms, said prayers, and learned Gaelic. At the time, life in Ireland seemed like a marvelous adventure. But our three years passed quickly, and now that part of my life seems like a foggy, green dream.

After Ireland, we moved to Pennsylvania. We had the mountains to remind us of Ireland (sort of) instead of the flat land I remembered from Indiana. But we had no sea, no blue waves of the ocean anywhere in sight. Again, I started a new school and

made new friends. This time it was a small, private Protestant school. (It's good to be well-rounded.) Driving a car with automatic transmission and on the right side of the road came back quickly to my parents. Shopping was easier with more and bigger stores and a greater variety of foods. But we had no more late-night visits from the neighbors, no more biscuits and tea at 10 P.M. People were too busy to socialize, it seemed. Occasional snowstorms, major and minor, were a welcome interruption during our winter weeks of school.

Now, after three years in Pennsylvania, we are packing the moving van again. We are headed for what seems like another foreign country—California. Dad says I can finish high school in California before he will accept another transfer. I don't know if I should be comforted or scared by that. Really. What will the schools be like in California? What will the weather be like? Will I live by the ocean or the mountains or neither or both?

What do I *hope* it will be like?

0-7696-3400-1 *Story Elements for Middle School Students*

The Traveler cont.

In the story on pages 18–19, the author tells about three places in which she has lived. Read each description below. Write *a, b,* or *c* to show which setting fits the description. Some descriptions fit more than one setting.

a. Indiana   **b.** Ireland   **c.** Pennsylvania

_____ 1. mountainous

_____ 2. flat

_____ 3. sometimes snowy

_____ 4. private school

_____ 5. public school

_____ 6. home school

_____ 7. religious school

_____ 8. close to the water

_____ 9. friendly neighbors

Contrast the author's Irish home with other homes in which she lived. (You will need to draw some of your own conclusions based on clues in the story.) List at least three things you think are different.

	Irish	American
10.	_____	_____
11.	_____	_____
12.	_____	_____

13. Which home do you think the writer preferred? Why?

_____

_____

14. How do you predict she will like California?

_____

15. The author used a lot of phrases in parentheses. Go back and read the story again, leaving out those words and phrases. How is the story different?

_____

_____

Why do you think the writer included those phrases?

_____

_____

16. Why do you think the writer's family moved so often?

_____

_____

What age was the author—

17. when she was learned she was moving to Ireland?

_____

18. when she moved to Pennsylvania?

_____

19. when she was moving to California?

_____

20. About how old will the author be before her dad will consider moving again?

_____

20

Words of Wisdom

Read each dialogue fragment below. Then write a more appropriate quote for each setting that is described.

1. An actor is about to audition. The lines he's memorized are:
"I'm pleased to meet you. Welcome to our town. Where is your new home?"

He thinks he's auditioning for a western, so this is how he plans to deliver the lines:

_____

_____

_____

2. Alas, he's actually auditioning for a daytime television soap opera. How should he say the lines now?

_____

_____

_____

3. Mr. Norgaur, everyone's favorite substitute teacher, has been assigned to teach kindergarten.

The principal wants Mr. Norgaur to explain to the children that they will all be checked for head lice that day. What does Mr. Norgaur say to the young students?

_____

_____

_____

4. At lunch time, kindergarten is over, but your teacher goes home ill. Now Mr. Norgaur must go through the entire head lice explanation again, to you and your classmates. What will he say this time?

_____

_____

5. The weather report predicts twenty-four inches of snow in the next twenty-four hours. Wendy, the new radio weather reporter, is very excited she is on duty to cover the storm.

Her first announcement reads as follows:

_____

_____

_____

6. The station manager takes hundreds of calls from hysterical listeners who are frightened by the first weather report. She asks Wendy to tone down her forecast and, with the next weather update, to give viewers information and advice to help them through the storm. This time her report reads as follows:

_____

_____

_____

21

The Boarder

Read the story and then answer the questions on page 23.

Simon's mom ran a boardinghouse. Ever since he could remember, Simon, along with his little sister, Zimmy, and his mom lived in the front half of their big home while other people lived in small apartments in the back and upstairs. Because he had grown up with it, Simon was accustomed to the noise of people walking around upstairs at all hours of the day and night, of "wallmates" pounding on the wall behind his bed, and of strangers hanging around on the big front porch.

Mom's boarders came from all over and came for many reasons. Dennis was one of Simon's favorite tenants. Dennis had come to live there six years ago when his elderly mother passed away. He had never before left home, even though he was thirty-two when his mother died. He had stayed in his childhood home, tenderly caring for his mother as her health declined and keeping things up around the house. People used to say, "Look at Dennis, dear man. There he is out mowing his mama's grass (or painting

her house or fixing her gutters or buying her groceries) when most men his age are out having fun with friends or finding a wife. God bless Dennis!"

Eventually Dennis's mama died. Dennis's mama left the house to her niece, Maureen. Simon still remembered how surprised everyone was at that news! The day the will was read, he'd heard that Maureen called Dennis, said she was arriving the next day, and told him he had twenty-four hours to vacate the house. So Dennis came to rent an apartment from Simon's mother.

Simon and Dennis spent time rocking and talking together on the big front porch. Their friendship went smoothly unless Simon asked too many questions. Once Simon signed for a package that came for Dennis by overnight express. It was a big, black envelope that arrived while Dennis was at the store. When Dennis returned, Simon gave him the envelope and hung around to see what it was and who sent it. But Dennis turned pale and went up to his room without saying a word. Another time Simon asked Dennis how he could pay his rent and buy his groceries since he never went to work. Dennis looked cold and again walked away.

Then one day Simon overheard an astonishing conversation. He and Zimmy were drinking milkshakes at Len's Diner. Three men in the corner booth were talking a bit too loudly. "If you ask me," hissed the first man, "we've played games with Dennis long enough. I say it's time for him to put up or shut up. If he's got something on us, let him produce it. Paying blackmail is for the birds."

The second man spoke up. "Well, Mac, we didn't ask you, and I say your idea stinks. I say we keep playing by his rules. If he has

     0-7696-3400-1 *Story Elements for Middle School Students*

The Boarder cont.

ROOMS FOR RENT

what he says he has, we're cooked. What do *you* say, Joe?"

Joe was the biggest man of the trio, with thick, dark hair. "Well, guys, here's what I think. I think both of your plans are rotten, and I have a better one of my own. There's a way to end the blackmail *and* end the risk that anyone will ever learn our secret. Let's wait until dark and pay ol' Dennis a visit at the boardinghouse. Catch my drift?"

The two men shifted uncomfortably in their seats. "Well, Joe, I have to admit you may be on to something there, but . . . well . . . ," one answered. Then the conversation grew hushed and intense. Simon could no longer hear what they said.

Zimmy spoke up, "Simon! Did you hear that? Do those men want to hurt Dennis? Isn't he your friend? He wouldn't do anything bad, would he? Will they come beat him up at our house? Should we tell Mom?"

"Shhhh, Zimmy! What are you thinking? We can't let those guys or anyone know what we just heard. I need some time to sort this thing out in my head. There are big risks to weigh and important choices to make here. Just give me a few minutes, please."

1. What conflict, or problem, does Simon face?

   _____

   _____

2. What are his options?

   _____

   _____

   _____

3. Which choice do you think is the best one?

   _____

   _____

4. For what reasons might Simon be reluctant to go to the police with the information he overheard at the diner?

   _____

   _____

5. Why do you think Dennis's mama did not leave her house to him in her will?

   _____

   _____

6. Finish the story. On another sheet of paper, write a brief ending that tells what Simon did and what happened to Dennis and to the three men.

0-7696-3400-1 *Story Elements for Middle School Students*

Choices

A conflict is a problem a story character must solve. In the conflicts described below, the characters must choose between two actions. Write the two choices on the lines. Put an asterisk next to the action you think the character should take. Then compare your answers with those of your classmates. Did everyone list the same two choices? Or did some think of additional choices? Do you all agree on the best choice?

Rob, Ashanti, and Kyle were each driving a van full of children on the ninety-minute trip from Kelsie's Preschool to the zoo. The drivers agreed that since Rob was the only one who knew the way, he should lead the caravan. Ashanti would follow him, and Kyle would follow her. Twenty minutes after departure, Ashanti realized Kyle was not behind her and she wasn't sure when she had lost him.

Ashanti's choices:

1. _____

   _____

2. _____

   _____

Mario had been saving for college since he was ten years old. It was the summer before his last year of high school. He was about to accept a good-paying summer job when his uncle phoned asking him to accompany him on a trip to Alaska. They would be gone for six weeks, driving and visiting relatives. They would travel through six states and many Canadian provinces, seeing places and wildlife that Mario had only imagined. They would meet relatives known to him only as names signed on cards his family received each Christmas.

Mario's choices:

3. _____

   _____

4. _____

   _____

Heidi's best friends, Alyssa and Glenna, had just invited her to go ice skating. She had only gone skating once before, and she'd had a wonderful time. Her parents never took her to do stuff like that. Heidi burst through the front door of her home, intending to ask her parents' permission. But before she could speak, she was enveloped in a big hug and mushy kisses. Oh, no! How could she have forgotten? Great-aunt Mildred from Idaho was visiting and had arranged to take Heidi's family out to eat. It promised to be a dreadfully boring evening, Heidi thought.

Heidi's choices:

5. _____

   _____

6. _____

   _____

0-7696-3400-1 *Story Elements for Middle School Students*

Lance Armstrong

Conflict

Read the story and answer the questions that follow it.

Lance Armstrong never gives up.

Armstrong is well known as a five-time Tour de France winner. However, his path to fame and success was not an easy one. Lance was born in 1971, in Plano, Texas. His mother was single, and money was tight. His mother later married Terry Armstrong, who adopted Lance.

Lance tried playing football, the most popular sport among boys in the area, but he wasn't very good at it. He played other sports and won the Iron Kids Triathlon at age 13, swimming, biking, and running to victory. Swimming and running fell away, and Armstrong was soon among the best teenage cyclists in the United States.

He placed fourteenth in the 1992 Olympic games. But he finished last in his first professional race the following year—so far last that only his determination kept him in the race and on the racing circuit. But tenacity paid off. At 22, he became the youngest road-racing world champion.

Lance was the world's highest-ranked bicyclist in October 1996—when disaster struck. He had testicular cancer—and it had spread to his lungs and brain. From the first, he declared his intention to beat the disease. And, from the first, he established

the Lance Armstrong Foundation to benefit cancer research and to help people with cancer. Through his own determination, with help from his family, and because of medical science, Lance survived two major surgeries and aggressive cancer treatments that damage the body while attacking the cancer. Incredibly, he returned to training just five months after his diagnosis.

Armstrong rejoined the racing circuit in 1998. In 1999, he proved that he was again the world's top cyclist, winning the Tour de France. This race covers over 2,100 rugged miles in twenty-two days! Lance won this competition again in 2000, then headed to the summer Olympics in Australia. While training, he was hit by a car and suffered broken bones in his back. He rode in the Olympics anyway, and his team won bronze medals for the United States.

Lance won three more consecutive Tour de France victories in 2001, 2002, and 2003. He was named Sports Illustrated Sportsman of the Year in 2002. Armstrong still counts his greatest victory as the win over cancer and still, through his foundation, financially supports cancer patients and cancer research. Even more than the financial support, Armstrong gives hope to people with cancer.

1. What was the biggest conflict, or problem, Lance Armstrong faced?

_____

2. What lesser obstacles has he faced?

_____

3. What has Lance given to others?

_____

4. Why did *Sports Illustrated* name Lance Sportsman of the Year?

_____

25

This Does Not Compute

Grandmother wrote to me just the other day.
And here is what she had to say:
"Dear Grandson, How long should it take
To learn this computer, for goodness' sake?

"You see, I try so hard to be
Caught up with all the technology.
I'm reading the manual. (It's three inches thick!)
I can't understand it, and it's making me sick.

"I'm learning about files, how to view and delete,
How to undo actions, to save and repeat.
But what I really want to know is how I can better
Write multiple copies of my own Christmas letter?

"For example, I like to greet Cousin Esther
Differently than her twin sister, Hester.
But the family news is essentially the same,
And the ends of the letters can all bear my name.

"Is it worth the hassle of files and such?
(Is learning all this just getting too much?)
Should I ask you, my very dear grandson,
Do you think tutoring me would be any fun?

"Just what is the chance that I'll ever learn
How to use this computer before I turn
A century old, or is it a lost cause?
If it is, I'll just give this to ol' Santa Claus!"

0-7696-3400-1 *Story Elements for Middle School Students*

Computing cont.

1. What problem does Grandmother have?

   _____

2. What feature of the computer does she most want to use?

   _____

3. What is her main purpose in writing the poetic letter to her grandson?

   _____

4. Do you think Grandmother should continue with the computer or give up learning to use it? Why or why not?

   _____

5. What line in the poem indicates that Grandmother might be willing to spend more time trying to learn the computer?

   _____

6. Is the poem set in the past, present, or future?

   _____

7. Is Grandmother's letter written in first, second, or third person?

   _____

8. The **theme** of a story or poem is the idea, viewpoint, or meaning that is found throughout the piece. Circle the letter for the best theme for "This Does Not Compute."

   a. Old people don't like what young people like.   c. Computers can save a lot of time.

   b. Christmas is a great time to write letters.   d. New technologies can be difficult to learn.

9. Think of another suitable title for this poem.

   _____

A Dirty Job

Read each paragraph of this story and answer the questions.

I think I have one of the dirtiest jobs in the world. But it's what I do best, and I love my job. Mind you, I also take a lot of abuse, and I can't stand that! Here's an example from the other day. It all started when Marcus drags me out of the closet. He pulls and tugs on my cord, which, of course, wears out my connection there. Why can't he use my nice, sturdy handle?

1. What object do you think is speaking?

_____

Well, anyway, Marcus plugs me in and pulls me into his bedroom. He clears a small area in the middle of the floor, where he wants to start this monumental task. Does he really expect me to clean up this mess? It's been far too long since he's brought me in here. I hope he is going to tackle one small area at a time.

2. How does the bedroom look?

_____

He turns me on and the fun begins. I swallow the broken bits of corn chips. I devour the tiny bits of scrap paper, and eventually, after several back-and-forth strokes, I suction up the grit, dirt, and sand that he's brought in on the bottom of his track shoes.

3. Underline the verbs in the paragraph above that describe the speaker's actions.

Help! I'm gasping for breath. What is suffocating me? Quickly, Marcus, turn me off. If you don't, I'm going to burn up. Marrrrrr….

4. What problem is the speaker having?

_____

5. What do you think caused the problem?

_____

Whew! I can breathe again. Thanks, Marcus! You really shouldn't leave your long, fringed winter scarf on the floor when you're using me. That could have been disastrous for both of us.

6. How do you think the problem was resolved?

_____

7. How can it be prevented from happening again?

_____

Marcus smells the burnt rubber in the air that came from the belt on my beater bar. He opens the window quickly, hoping to air out his room before his mother smells it. He wraps up my cord and very respectfully returns me to the closet. I hope he's learned something today!

8. What should Marcus have learned today?

_____

9. Underline the climax.

28

     0-7696-3400-1 *Story Elements for Middle School Students*

Get Relevant, Man!

Read each paragraph. Decide on the **main idea** or **story synopsis**. Then look for three supporting ideas or subplot elements. Write these in the blanks. Finally, cross out the irrelevant details that do not relate to the main plot.

Constantine is planning a Fourth of July celebration like none the town has ever done before. The village will be two-hundred years old this year, and the citizenry want to mark it with a big bang! The mayor will lead a parade, beginning at 10:30 A.M. Last year's parade started at the same time. First Church will hold a chicken barbecue. Mrs. Fisher, who is 69, will be the church's head cook. No one has chosen an official photographer yet. The grand day will end with fireworks over the river at 11 P.M.

1. Main idea: _____

_____

Supporting ideas:

a. _____

b. _____

c. _____

Kathleen and Jason enjoy going to yard sales because they never know what they might find. It's also a relaxing way to spend time together. Last week they went to one sale across the street and another three blocks away. In one day, they found an almost-new playpen for their baby, some shiny hubcaps for their sports car, and a great polka-dot purse Kathleen's mother was sure to love. Kathleen's mom looks forward to them bringing the baby over for a visit. Their best find last week was a mahogany bookcase that cost only $10!

2. Plot: _____

_____

Subplots:

a. _____

b. _____

c. _____

The bridge was amazing. I'd been over some big overpasses on interstates but never one that spanned so much beautiful clear blue water. Seeing the magnificent Mackinac Bridge made the six-hour drive from Toledo worthwhile. While on vacation, we often stop at scenic lookout points. After crossing the bridge, we entered a wonderful wilderness world, Michigan's Upper Peninsula. Not far from the highway we could see vast stands of timber and sometimes deer and elk. Lumberjacks who live in the UP like to eat a meat and potato dish called a pasty. Yum!

3. Plot: _____

_____

Subplots:

a. _____

b. _____

c. _____

29

The Knock

Read this story opening. Then answer the questions on page 31.

I woke up with a start and looked at the clock. It read 2:32 A.M. Thinking I must have been awakened by a bad dream, I rolled over and tried to go back to sleep. That's when I clearly heard someone pounding at the door and a very heavy rainfall beating down on the roof.

"Let me in!" the voice urged. "Please, I need to come in—now!"

I scrambled for my robe and went barefooted down the stairs to the front hallway. I peered through the peephole and saw a stranger with a long gray beard and worn clothes. I wasn't sure what to do; I'd never seen this man before. But how could I leave him outside—in the heavy rain and at this hour? Cautiously, I opened the door.

"Thank goodness I was able to wake you, Wes. It must be quite a surprise to find me at your door in the middle of the night."

"I'll say," I replied. I could have added, *It would be a surprise to find you here any time because I have no idea who you are!* But I didn't. I just calmly let the man in.

"Say, sonny, I reckon it's possible you don't even remember me. I am honestly and truly your Uncle Abe, your grandma's brother, on your mom's side. Just so you know I'm not pullin' your leg, I can tell you that your mom's maiden name was Peterson and your grandma's maiden name was Russell."

I couldn't argue with anything Uncle Abe said because I didn't even know my grandma's maiden name. I knew he had my mom's name right. I had just last month

gone through all of her documents after the lawyer read her will.

"Let's get down to business," Uncle Abe continued. "I just arrived on the bus. I've been riding across country for three days. I know I'm dying of cancer, and I won't be long in this world. Close as I can figure, you're my nearest kin. In my baggage, I have some interestin' belongings. I hope to sell this diamond brooch, which belonged to my mother, to pay for my final weeks of medical care. But this old pocket watch and porcelain locket are yours. I wanted to deliver them before it was too late and they fell into some ol' government stash somewhere."

I persuaded Uncle Abe to spend the rest of the night on the couch. I could deal with the sale of the brooch and the medical arrangements in the morning, I thought. I needed to get some sleep, and, more importantly, I needed to take in everything Uncle Abe had said and figure out if he was telling the truth. Come to think of it, how did I even know all my stuff was safe with him down there? How did I know if I was safe?

     0-7696-3400-1 *Story Elements for Middle School Students*

The Knock cont.

In this story starter, one main event occurs: Wes finds a stranger at his door. But several small events occur within the big event. These details help provide clues about what will happen next, and they build excitement as the major events unfold. List the minor points of action in order.

1. _____

2. _____

3. _____

4. _____

5. _____

6. _____

7. _____

8. Why do you think Wes was hesitant to let Uncle Abe in?

_____

_____

9. Does Wes know for sure that the stranger's story is true? If not, how can he find out?

_____

_____

10. It seems that the climax (or moment of highest suspense) is just about to happen. The full title of the story is "The Knock That Changed My Life." Write a brief ending to the story that fits that title.

_____

_____

_____

_____

_____

_____

_____

31

The Picnic

Read "The Picnic," then follow the instructions on page 33.

It was the first weekend of the summer, and the Posadas intended to enjoy it. After an early breakfast, Mom and Alicia made a pile of ham sandwiches while Ricky and Dad gathered up the life jackets and inner tubes. As everyone picked out a favorite piece of fresh fruit, Mom noticed that the peaches had spoiled, the bananas were green, and the apples were brown. So they skipped the fruit. Sandwiches, cans of soda, and big blue ice packs were carefully packed in the foam cooler.

On the two-hour trip to the beach and picnic area, it started to rain. "Oh, no!" cried Mom. "Our picnic will be ruined!"

"Don't give up just yet," replied Dad. "We still have an hour to drive, and it looks like just a passing shower."

Unhappily, Dad was wrong. The sky grew darker and darker the farther they drove. With the windshield wipers going full speed, Dad could barely see the road. Finally, he pulled over and waited for the rain to let up.

Before the rain diminished, however, great chunks of hail pelted the car. From the backseat, Ricky cheered. "Hey! This must be what they call golf-ball-sized hail. Cool!" Mom just groaned and closed her eyes.

Eventually the sky cleared, and Dad pulled back on the road. *Thump, thump, thump!* They all heard the noise from the left rear side of the car.

"Well, guys," Dad pronounced. "It looks like another delay. I think we have a flat tire. I must have hit something sharp when I pulled

off the road." Alicia, glad for a chance to get out and walk around, offered to help Dad with the jack and spare tire.

"Will we ever get there?" asked Mom. Dad assured her they would.

He was right. About four hours after leaving home, the Posadas drove into the state park. Dad was thrilled when he pulled up at the entrance and saw that no one was there to collect admission fees. Remembering he was driving on a flimsy spare, he carefully maneuvered over and around several speed bumps. The next sign the family saw startled them into momentary speechlessness.

Large signs read No Swimming Allowed. Around the picnic area, signs read Do Not Loiter and We Are Not Responsible for Your Safety.

After the surprise wore off, the children demanded, "What's this all about? Why can't we swim? Is the water polluted or something? What's the safety problem at the picnic tables?"

"I'm sorry I can't answer any of your

32

The Picnic cont.

questions," Dad answered quietly. "I have no idea what's going on, but this doesn't look like a place we want to be. Where to now, Mom?"

Just then a large, dark creature arose from the lake. The mammoth creature placed two huge, heavy black feet on the shore. Two more slimy appendages waved like arms as the beast started toward the car. It opened a wide, tooth-filled mouth and blinked huge green eyes at the Posadas.

The entire family shrieked and screamed as Dad spun a doughnut and headed out of the parking lot as fast as the speed bumps allowed. After the last speed bump, the kids dared to look behind them. "Whew!" exclaimed Ricky. "Looks like the Thing stopped chasing us."

"This picnic was doomed from the start," moaned Mom. "I guess next time we'll just stop for burgers."

List, in order, ten of the central events of the story. Rate the degree of suspense of each event. Use 1 = low suspense and 5 = high suspense (or the story's climax). Be sure to use the full range of numbers.

Event	Rating (1–5)
1. _____	_____
2. _____	_____
3. _____	_____
4. _____	_____
5. _____	_____
6. _____	_____
7. _____	_____
8. _____	_____
9. _____	_____
10. _____	_____

0-7696-3400-1 *Story Elements for Middle School Students*

Fairy Tale

Read these scrambled events from a well-known fairy tale.
1) Rearrange the words so each sentence makes sense.
2) Write the sentences in order on page 35. Some events
   are supplied to give you clues to the rest of the story.
3) Circle the number of the sentence that marks the climax
   of the story.

a. gingerbread, The began hungry eat cottage of to it children was made and the.

_____

b. poor had The food family very was and no.

_____

c. invited in woman the and door a appeared Suddenly old an at meal for them.

_____

d. delighted his to see woodcutter was children The again.

_____

e. lived after And happily they ever.

_____

f. tricked pushed the her witch Gretel One into day and oven the hot.

_____

g. wife edge A lived with woodcutter of two forest on the children a his and.

_____

h. way last The found their at home children.

_____

i. realized wicked planned Soon the she eat really witch was to who children a them.

_____

j. agreed reluctantly the woodcutter Against better very judgment, his.

_____

k. stable freed Gretel brother her from Next, the.

_____

l. them lose suggested The forest in mother the they let children the die and there.

_____

34

Fairy Tale cont.

1. _____

2. The boy's name was Hansel, and the girl's name was Gretel.

3. _____

4. _____

5. _____

6. While the children were trying to find their way out of the forest, they came upon a cottage.

7. _____

8. _____

9. _____

10. The witch locked Hansel in the stable and forced Gretel to feed him and fatten him up for the witch's meal.

11. _____

12. _____

13. Then she scooped up the witch's jewels to take home to her father.

14. _____

15. They learned their mother had died.

16. _____

17. Thanks to the witch's jewels they were never poor again.

18. _____

Proverbs

A theme is the main point the author tries to make in a piece of writing. Proverbs by Benjamin Franklin and others provide great story themes. Read each story synopsis. Then match it to the appropriate proverb by writing the letter of the proverb next to the story. There are extra proverbs.

a. Necessity is the mother of invention.
b. A stitch in time saves nine.
c. You can lead a horse to water, but you can't make it drink.
d. Don't count your chickens until they've hatched.

e. Actions speak louder than words.
f. People who live in glass houses shouldn't throw stones.
g. The grass always looks greener on the other side of the fence.

_____ **1.** Queen Agatha was jealous of her sister, the Queen of Waterford. *Why does she have all the luck?* Agatha asked herself. *When she was engaged to be married to William, no one thought he'd ever amount to anything. Now, suddenly, here he is, King of Waterford!* Agatha had thought she herself was destined for the easy, luxurious life when she became betrothed to Henry. But alas, Henry had gambled away the family fortune.

_____ **2.** Mike flipped open the new MallParcus catalog. "Mom, can I have this sweater? It's perfect for me!" he exclaimed.

His mother said, "Mike, you know we don't have extra money for extravagant things right now. You already have plenty of nice sweaters."

"Aw, come on, Mom. I can pay for it myself with the money I'll make babysitting for the Lamberts. I promise I'll pay you back."

Mike's mother finally agreed. She ordered the sweater online and charged it to her credit card. She instructed

Mike, "It will be about a month before the credit card bill comes. When it does, you will pay me for the sweater so I can pay off the bill."

The sweater came, and Mike really liked it. The bill came too, but Mike didn't have the money to pay it. His mother wanted to know why.

"Well, Mom, Mrs. Lambert was calling me every Friday night to sit for Lauren and Tyler, and she paid me $15 each time. But the Lamberts went on vacation for two weeks, and Tyler was sick another Friday, so I went there only once during the whole month. I'm really sorry. I can only pay you $15 of the $59 I owe you."

His mother said quietly, "Mike, I was telling the truth when I told you there's no extra money right now. So $44 of the money we had budgeted for you to play soccer will have to go for the credit card

36

   0-7696-3400-1 *Story Elements for Middle School Students*

Proverbs cont.

bill instead. I'm sorry. You won't be able to play."

Mike couldn't speak. Not play soccer? The new sweater didn't seem so perfect any more.

___ **3.** Lexie's parents were not around enough to make sure Lexie had food to eat and clean clothes to wear. They certainly did not make sure their daughter went to school or did her homework. So it was no surprise when Lexie failed classes and got into trouble. She stayed out past curfew and stole things from the corner store. She was caught and sentenced to a juvenile detention home.

When she had served her time, the court placed Lexie with the Kinneys, a foster family eager to share their home and love with her. Lexie knew that to remain with them, she must follow their house rules and get home on time every night. At first, she seemed happy to comply. Soon, however, she got in touch with her old friends. Then she broke curfew three times in one week and lied about where she'd been. The Kinneys were upset.

"Doesn't she see," Mrs. Kinney cried to the probation officer, "that we're offering her everything—a clean home, her own room, plenty of food, and a family who cares about her? Why is she throwing it all away?"

___ **4.** Student-body elections were just two days away. Ashley wanted to be elected president more than she'd ever wanted anything before. She found a way gain a last minute edge on Roger, her toughest opponent. Samantha told Ashley that last year Mrs. McQueen, the English teacher, had caught Roger cheating on a quiz. (He got a zero on the quiz and had detention for a week.)

At the pre-election assembly, Ashley spoke first—and disclosed Roger's wrongdoing to the entire student body. Giggling and whispers went through the auditorium when Roger stood to speak. His first words reminded everyone that Ashley, just last month, had been caught cheating on a math test.

5. Now, on a separate piece of paper, use one of the unused proverbs to write a brief story synopsis of your own.

37

Spin Action

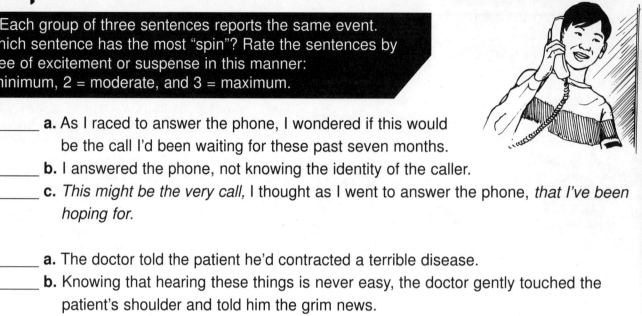

Each group of three sentences reports the same event. Which sentence has the most "spin"? Rate the sentences by degree of excitement or suspense in this manner: 1 = minimum, 2 = moderate, and 3 = maximum.

1. _____ **a.** As I raced to answer the phone, I wondered if this would be the call I'd been waiting for these past seven months.

   _____ **b.** I answered the phone, not knowing the identity of the caller.

   _____ **c.** *This might be the very call,* I thought as I went to answer the phone, *that I've been hoping for.*

2. _____ **a.** The doctor told the patient he'd contracted a terrible disease.

   _____ **b.** Knowing that hearing these things is never easy, the doctor gently touched the patient's shoulder and told him the grim news.

   _____ **c.** Dr. Schut hesitated before going into the exam room, wondering how he could ever tell Ken, his best buddy since second grade, that he probably had only a few months to live.

3. _____ **a.** Yesenia carefully untied the bow of the tiny, delicately wrapped present.

   _____ **b.** Yesenia unwrapped the package.

   _____ **c.** Yesenia gently shook the gift, listening for any clues to its content, before removing the paper corner by corner.

4. _____ **a.** "Just put your hands above your head," the police officer said firmly.

   _____ **b.** "I'm not messing around with you! Hands over your head, or else!" ordered the chief of police.

   _____ **c.** The police officer told the suspect to put her hands in the air.

5. _____ **a.** The python wrapped its body around the unsuspecting mouse.

   _____ **b.** The python saw a mouse and decided to eat it.

   _____ **c.** When the python spied the mouse, he sprang out of nowhere and trapped his prey.

6. _____ **a.** As a writer, I don't often lack for ideas, but this week was the exception.

   _____ **b.** With an imagination that usually bursts at its seams, I floundered all week searching for any bit of inspiration I could find—anywhere.

   _____ **c.** It's been really tough lately for me to find ideas to write about.

38

Name _____ Date _____

Which Person?

Below are ten short paragraphs. In each blank, write 1 if the paragraph is written in first person, 2 if it is written in second person, and 3 if it is written in third person.

____ **1.** You are the luckiest person on the face of the earth! You have long blond hair, purple eyes, and green skin. On your feet, you actually have six toes!

____ **2.** I, on the other hand, am rather boring in comparison. I am 5'4" with brown hair and brown eyes. I think I am average in almost every way.

____ **3.** On the day Mom gave birth, she told Grandma that she never loved anything more than she loved the baby in her arms.

____ **4.** I know she still loves me today, but sometimes it doesn't feel like it. When she makes me come home at ten o'clock and won't let me ride in the car with someone she doesn't know, I feel like she's being too strict.

____ **5.** Your mom, on the other hand, lets you go to the Green-Skinned People's Coffeehouse until 3 A.M., even on school nights. You are allowed to watch anything on television, and your dad never asks to see your homework.

____ **6.** Mrs. English asked Jamie, Jacob, and all purple-eyed people to put their math problems on the board. Jamie and Jacob did a great job, but the others did not.

____ **7.** Mr. Math asked Rhoda and Mary and all green-skinned people to write their vocabulary words on the board. Of that group, only Rhoda and Mary were prepared.

____ **8.** Do you have any idea why the principal called your mother? Do you think he's overreacting to rumors he may have heard about you?

____ **9.** When you found out you weren't moving on to high school with the rest of the class but were staying in junior high one more year, you were really disappointed.

____ **10.** We begged, we pleaded, we prayed, and we crossed our fingers, but nothing changed the outcome. We all agreed that ninth grade wouldn't be the same without you.

0-7696-3400-1 *Story Elements for Middle School Students*

Neutral News Clips?

A guiding principle of news writing is to report facts without offering opinions. Read these excerpts from news stories. Then choose the statement that best describes the point of view revealed in each story. If the writer is not objectively reporting the facts, underline the words in the story that reveal the writer's personal viewpoint, or *bias*.

1. Three feet of snow fell today in less than three hours, according to our weather service. Such heavy snowfalls, although rare here, show the need for improved snow removal equipment. Also, more money must be available to pay overtime for city street workers. The snowfall was the heaviest since the blizzard of 1978.

   The writer is

   a. objectively reporting the facts.
   b. believes the city council has not budgeted correctly.
   c. enjoys the heavy snowfall.

2. Clint Richmond was elected overwhelmingly in yesterday's presidential election. He received 306 electoral votes, 36 more than the 270 needed to be elected. In the popular vote, Richmond received 59 percent of the vote, while 32 percent of the vote went to contender Leah Spring, and 7 percent of the popular vote was won by Mike Vincent.

   The writer is

   a. objectively reporting the facts.
   b. pleased that Richmond won the election.
   c. thinks the race should have been closer.

3. The new HomeHelp store opened today amid some controversy about its hiring policies. The store's owner cut a red ribbon while demonstrators carried sloppily written signs that read, HomeHelp Hates Women! HomeHelp Didn't Help Me! and This Store Only Hires Men. Understandably, the demonstrators drew jeers from the crowd gathered to shop at the new store. The store will provide more than one hundred much-needed jobs and already has hired a generous percentage of women.

   The writer is

   a. objectively reporting the facts.
   b. in favor of HomeHelp and its hiring practices.
   c. believes HomeHelp is unfair to women.

4. Only 425 fans attended last night's high school football game. Residents seem apathetic to our teenagers and their interests. Ticket sales from all high school sports brought in just 50 percent of expected revenues last year. This further indicates the public's lack of interest in high school students. Perhaps if more adults in the community supported our high school athletes, the dropout rate would decrease.

   The writer is

   a. objectively reporting the facts.
   b. apathetic about high school sports.
   c. believes people in the community should be more interested in high school sports.

40

0-7696-3400-1 *Story Elements for Middle School Students*

Your Analysis

Identify the characters, the conflict, and the setting for each story starter. Write your answers on another piece of paper.

Tiffany rummaged the shed behind her grandmother's house, on a day when she could think of nothing to do. She found rusty screwdrivers, almost-empty paint cans, garden tools, and outdated seeds.

Just as she turned to leave the shed, a tidy, tied-up box tucked away on an upper shelf caught her eye. *Maybe there's a forgotten treasure inside*, she thought. She cautiously stepped onto a rickety stepladder. She just needed it for a quick reach. Bam! Down she went into a box of sharp, rusty tools.

Tiffany couldn't get up. She hadn't told her grandmother where she was going. How long would it take someone to find her?

1. Describe the character in one sentence.

2. Describe the setting.

3. What is the conflict?

Pirate Perciville was upset. Hadn't he always taught his crew that when they robbed ships on the high seas, they should do so with honor and dignity? Ever since James joined the crew there had been trouble. James seemed to think it was proper to frighten the women and children aboard victimized ships. Yesterday, he had ripped a necklace off of a frightened little girl! Perciville could still see the terror in her eyes. No, sir. He just couldn't allow James to keep raiding in such a violent way. There was, after all, a *right* way to be a pirate.

4. Name and describe the characters.

5. What is the conflict?

6. How might the conflict be resolved?

Ryan always wanted his own way. Cody, his younger brother, was tired of being bossed around. On Saturday, Cody came to the end of his rope. He'd put up with Ryan pulling his hair, knocking over his cereal, and changing the television channel during his favorite show. However, he was not going to put up with Ryan hiding his favorite video game in his room!

7. Name and describe the characters.

8. What is the setting?

9. What is the conflict?

Misfits

Read each paragraph carefully to find what doesn't belong. Something may not match the setting, actions may not fit the character, and so on. Circle the misfit(s) in each paragraph. In the lines below the stories, tell why you circled each item.

1. It was a dark and stormy night, not fit for human or horse. But Mrs. Landis was in labor, and Doc Harvey knew he must make the three-mile trek into the country regardless of the weather. He hooked Buck, his favorite horse, to his dependable black buggy. He prayed that the metal buggy wheels would slog through the thick mud that surely would be on the dirt road that led to the Landis farm.

When he arrived at the farm, he was greeted by Mr. Landis, who had just finished cleaning the milking machine. Doc was grateful there would be another adult around, as this delivery might be a hard one. Two hours later, when there was still no sign of the baby, Doc decided to call it a night. He told Mr. Landis to call him at home if he needed him.

_____

_____

_____

2. Jeremy sure knew how to get a laugh. While Tom was the one students went to when they needed help with geometry, Jeremy was the first one to be invited to a party. He always drew a crowd at the lunch tables as kids gathered to hear about his latest pranks and jokes. Today, Tom decided he would ignore Jeremy's

table rather than try to fit in or pretend to laugh at Jeremy's goofy behavior.

Then suddenly, Tom looked up and there was Chloe, *the* most gorgeous girl in the entire school, joining *him*. What should he say? How could he start a conversation? Chloe took charge before Tom could think what to do. She started by asking him to the dance on Friday, and she ended by telling him how smart she thought he was. Before he could reply, Mrs. Cook called him up to the chalkboard to give his solution to the day's brainteaser.

_____

_____

0-7696-3400-1 *Story Elements for Middle School Students*

Misfits cont.

_____   _____

3. "Come right on in, fellas!" Mr. Clancy greeted the two boys warmly as they entered his candy shop. "What'll it be today? Licorice sticks? Gumdrops? Taffy?" Mr. Clancy was getting old, but his mind was still sharp as a tack. He always remembered his regular customers, and he could still add prices and make change without a calculator.

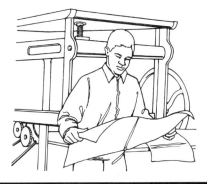

"I'm almost broke, sir, so I think I'll just take two of your nickel gumballs and five of your popcorn-flavored jelly beans," replied Jonathan, remembering that the jelly beans were a penny a piece. He handed Mr. Clancy a quarter.

The shopkeeper quickly bagged Jonathan's requests and rang up the sale on his antique cash register. He gave him a nickel in change and winked at Tim. "Looks like you're next!" he smiled.

Before Tim could make his request, a delivery driver walked in with two large cartons. "Hey, there, Verl! I'm sure glad to get this shipment. Why don't you set those boxes over in the corner by the lawn and garden tools. I'll sign your invoice and let you run along. I'm sure you have more stops yet today," the storeowner finished. Then he turned again to Tim, who promptly requested more nickel gumballs and penny jelly beans.

_____

_____

4. I had just finished another week of work. It would be so nice not to have to worry about all of the deadlines, I dreamed. It was hard to imagine what kind of life that would be. After all, I'd been working at the newspaper for half of my life, and I could practically do the typesetting in my sleep—large 24- or 36-point type for headlines, sometimes all caps; small italics for picture captions; proofs to the editor by 5:00 A.M.; changes by 5:45; presses rolling by 6:00; presses filled with ink and a fresh roll of paper before running the Sunday pages; and the letters cleaned after each day's run, then put back in the proper spaces in the wooden drawers. Everything went by the clock and the calendar.

Speaking of clocks, the alarm on my watch is going off. It's 4:25 P.M.. Oh, no! I'm late. The alarm was to remind me to leave home right now to go to the train station to meet my cousin who's been traveling all week from Sacramento. She'll be visiting for a month. I'm not even home. Drat! I guess she'll have to wait. She'll understand. She always does.

_____

_____

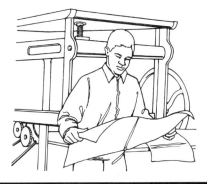

43

Diagnosis

Read the story. Then answer the questions on page 45.

I woke up on the morning of June 1, 1989, with a numb toe. I thought it was still "asleep." I shook it, jumped on it, walked on it, and rubbed it, but nothing changed. By the next day, my whole foot was numb. By the end of the week, the numbness had spread up my leg and to my other foot.

By August 1, I had the diagnosis. After two months of medical tests, I suppose I was relieved to have a name for my very real problem. At least then I knew it wasn't all in my mind. But I felt as though I had run into
a brick wall when the doctor told me I had multiple sclerosis.

Before that summer, I had been reasonably healthy and active. I was thirty-one, was happily married, and had two young children. I kept the books for our small business. I volunteered at church and mowed the lawn. I sewed clothes for all four of us. I canned peaches and made my own pickles. My biggest concerns had been paying the bills and keeping my children safe. I was content.

The brick-wall feeling remained with me for several days. What would MS mean for me? Would I be in a wheelchair? Would I be able to keep up all of my previous activities? How would my husband handle my illness? But all of those questions seemed unimportant compared to this one: Would I be able to be the kind of mother I really wanted to be?

That summer was fourteen years ago. My husband and I have now been married twenty-one years. My son is seventeen and ready for his senior year of high school. He is

tenderhearted, generous, and an honors student. My daughter is fifteen. She's multitalented, brilliant, and helpful. I guess I didn't do too badly, did I?

Multiple sclerosis has definitely changed my life. I do not do everything I want to because I don't have the energy. I don't can peaches, make pickles, and sew clothes. I can't be out in the sun. Sometimes I limp, and, yes, occasionally I do use a wheelchair. That numb feeling is now permanent on half of my body.

But on days when I couldn't run outside and play with my children, I could still hold them on my lap and read to them. I learned I could *be* mom even when I couldn't *do* all the typical "mom" things. My children have learned to be caring and helpful because of my illness. I have learned how to treat and live with the disease. And brick by brick, that wall I crashed into in 1989, the wall of the fear of the unknown, has been demolished. I am still content—usually.

0-7696-3400-1 *Story Elements for Middle School Students*

Diagnosis cont.

1. How does the author measure the success of her life?

_____

2. With what problems has the diagnosis presented her?

_____

3. What information is included about the setting?

_____

4. Why do you think the author wrote this story?

_____

5. Why do you think there is no information in the story about the cause of multiple sclerosis and the medical treatments for it?

_____

6. Complete this character web for the biography "Diagnosis."

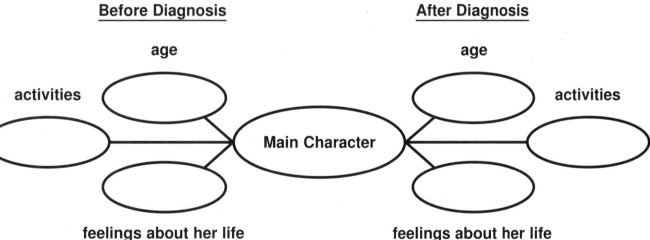

Before Diagnosis   **After Diagnosis**

age   age

activities   activities

Main Character

feelings about her life   feelings about her life

7. Describe what the author means by the "brick-wall" feeling? What other name does she give it near the end of the story?

_____

8. How has the brick wall been "demolished"?

_____

9. How does the author subtlely admit she still has fears and misses the things she used to do?

_____

45

Answer Key

General Genres . . . . p. 4
1. historical fiction
2. fantasy
3. realistic fiction
4. science fiction

Common Traits . . . . p. 5
Answers may vary.
1. a, b, c
2. c, e
3. c, d, e
4. a, b, c, f
5. f
6. a, b, c, d, e
7. d, f
8. c, d, e
9. a, b
10. a, b, c, e

Finishing Fits . . . . p. 6
Answers may vary.
1. historical fiction, biography
2. science fiction, mystery
3. mystery, autobiography
4. autobiography, realistic fiction
5. poetry, tall tale, folktale
6. folktale, realistic fiction

What Did You Say? . . . . p. 7
1. E
2. T
3. E
4. F
5. E
6. F
7. E
8. T
9. E
10. E
11. F
12. T
13. E
14. F
15. E
16. T

Who Says? . . . . p. 8
1. a, b, d, e, f
2. c, d, e
3. a, c, d
4. a, c, d, e
5. a, e

As You Speak . . . . p. 9
3.–14. Answers will vary.

The Attic . . . . p. 11
1. Dad, Susie King Taylor, Grandma Dolly
2. Miranda. Some of the sentences that could be underlined: "Whatever," Miranda added.
   . . . and Miranda reluctantly bringing up the rear; Five minutes into the task Miranda announced she was finished. "I'm throwing all of this stuff into a garbage bag, and then I'm done," she grumbled.
3. Matt
4. an amusement park
5. Susie King Taylor
6. They are siblings, or brother and sisters.
7. Answers may vary. Actual meaning is walked without apparent plan, wandered.

8. Miranda. She found something in the attic that interested her, something that had meaning for her.
9. Answers may include leading the charge, reluctantly bringing up the rear, grumbled, replied sarcastically, traipsed, whistled, and teasingly
10. Answers will vary.

Musical Mayhem . . . . p. 12
Instruments played first: Betsy, guitar; Justin, drums; Bryce, trombone; Angela, trumpet; Vince, saxophone; and Sarah, keyboard.

Instruments played second: Betsy, guitar; Justin, saxophone; Bryce, drums; Angela, trumpet; Vince, trombone; and Sarah, keyboard.

Dialogue Details . . . . p. 13
1. the king
2. the king's page
3. Yoman
4. b, c
5. the reporter
6. the President
7. the Vice President
8. the President
9. Dr. Ryan, female; the Vice President, male
10. the reporter and the President
11. Rudy and Toby
12. Misty and Zoe
13. Misty is probably a dog, and Zoe is probably a cat.
14. a, d

Role Play . . . . p. 14
1. e
2. b
3. d
4. i
5. g
6. a
7. j
8. c
9. f
10. h

Time and Place . . . . p. 15
1. midnight, deserted island
2. lunch hour, busy street
3. first day of school, school bus stop
4. Christmas, hospital
5. during a job interview, swimming pool
6. soccer practice, gymnasium
7. sunrise, cafeteria

The Storyteller . . . . p. 17
Answers may vary.
1. Africa
2. dry season/rainy season; baked earth; leopards and camels; the frogs came from Egypt, which is on the African continent
3. The storytelling happened "today."
4. The animal fable happened "many, many years ago."
5. a. hot, dry, sunny, hard, brown
   b. green, wet, lush, muddy
6. a difficult situation, a dilemma
7. yarn spinner, minstrel, narrator, teller of tales, grand fabler

The Traveler . . . . pp. 18–20
1.–14. Answers may vary.
1. b, c
2. a
3. a, c
4. c
5. a, b
6. b
7. b
8. b
9. b

Irish
10. hot water had to be turned on
11. one toilet
12. stone wall around house
American
10. hot water was always on
11. more than one toilet
12. no stone wall
13. Ireland; friendly neighbors, beautiful scenery
14. She will probably like some things about California and dislike other things.
15. The phrases give more information about how the writer feels about the facts she's including. It makes the article more interesting.
16. because of her father's job
17. eight
18. eleven
19. fourteen
20. about eighteen, or after she graduates from high school

Words of Wisdom . . . . p. 21
Answers will vary. Here are sample answers for the first two scenarios.
1. "Howdy there, partner. It's a pleasure to meet ya. Did you just ride into town? Would ya like to set a spell and shake the dust off your feet? Where you reckonin' on putting down yer stakes?"

0-7696-3400-1 *Story Elements for Middle School Students*

Answer Key

2. "Oh, I am so relieved to see you. You just can't imagine what a horrible time I've had without you. Please say you're staying here. You are buying a home here, right? Please tell me where it is, and please tell me it's nearby!"

The Boarder .... p. 23
1. Simon must decide whether to act on what he's heard.
2. He can pretend he didn't hear anything and hope the three men decided not to pay Dennis a visit. He can tell his mother. He can tell the police. He can tell Dennis what he's heard and warn him to go away for a while.
3. Answers will vary.
4. Since Dennis is Simon's friend, he may be hesitant to report Dennis as a possible blackmailer. He may not want to cause his mother any worry since the three men might simply keep quiet and do nothing right away.
5. Answers will vary. Maybe she knew he was a blackmailer and didn't approve of that. Maybe Dennis had already received a large inheritance from his father or some other relative.
6. Answers will vary.

Choices .... p. 24
1. Ashanti could continue to follow Rob, hoping Kyle eventually finds them.
2. She could pull over, turn around, and try to find Kyle. If she pulls over, she probably hopes Rob will notice and pull over too.
3. Mario could drive to Alaska.
4. He could stay home and accept the summer job.
5. Heidi could go out with her family and explain to her friends that she already had other plans she'd forgotten about.
6. She could go out with her friends and hope that her family understood.

Lance Armstrong .... p. 25
1. cancer
2. money was tight; not being able to play football; losing his first professional race; broken bones; grueling races
3. role model, money, hope
4. He won the Tour de France five years in a row.

Computing .... p. 27
Answers may vary.
1. She's trying to learn how to use her computer.
2. word processing
3. to ask how long it will take her to learn the computer
4. Answers will vary.
5. "Do you think tutoring me would be any fun?"
6. present
7. first person
8. d
9. Answers will vary.

A Dirty Job .... p. 28
1. The object is a vacuum cleaner, but answers may vary.
2. very messy
3. swallow, devour, suction
4. It can't get air.
5. Something large is probably caught in the hose or floor attachment.
6. Marcus probably saw that something was caught and pulled it out of the vacuum cleaner.
7. by keeping the vacuum away from large objects that might get sucked up into it
8. to be more careful when using the vacuum cleaner
9. Help! I'm gasping for breath. What is suffocating me?

Get Relevant, Man! .... p. 29
1. Main idea: Constantine is planning a Fourth of July celebration with many different events. Supporting ideas: a. There will be a parade. b. There will be a chicken barbecue. c. There will be fireworks.
Irrelevant details: Last year's parade also started at the same time. Mrs. Fisher, who is 69, will be the church's head cook. No one has chosen an official photographer yet.
2. Plot: Kathleen and Jason enjoy going to yard sales. Subplots: a. It's also a relaxing way to spend time together. b. They found a playpen, hubcaps, and a purse. c. They found a mahogany bookcase for only $10. Irrelevant details: Last week they went to one yard sale across the street and another one three blocks away. Kathleen's mom looks forward to them bringing the baby for a visit.

3. Plot: I enjoyed my first-ever visit to the Mackinac Bridge. Subplots: a. We had driven six hours to get to the bridge. b. After crossing the bridge, we drove on into the Upper Peninsula. c. The Upper Peninsula was a wonderful wilderness world with timber and wildlife. Irrelevant details: While on vacation, we often stop at scenic lookout points. Lumberjacks who live in the UP like to eat a meat and potato dish called a pasty. Yum!

The Knock .... p. 31
1. Wes woke up suddenly and heard a pounding at the door.
2. Wes went downstairs and discovered a stranger standing outside.
3. Wes decided to let the man come in.
4. The man tells Wes that he's his great-uncle.
5. Uncle Abe reveals the purpose of his trip.
6. Uncle Abe spends the night on Wes's couch.
7. Wes goes back to bed and thinks about everything he's learned.
8. because he'd never seen the man before
9. No. He could ask to see some sort of identification, or he could locate family historical documents.
10. Answers will vary.

The Picnic .... p. 33
Ratings and exact events may vary. The climax is the emergence of the creature from the water.
1. The family packed a picnic lunch. 1
2. They drove toward the park. 2
3. It started to rain. 3
4. Dad pulled off the road and it hailed. 4
5. They had a flat tire. 3
6. Dad and Alicia changed the tire. 1
7. They arrived at the park and entered it. 3
8. They read the warning signs. 4
9. A creature emerged from the lake. 5 (climax)
10. The family turned around and drove away. 4

Fairy Tale .... pp. 34–35
Here are the solved sentences in the correct sequence. The order of the words in the sentences may vary.

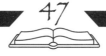

47

0-7696-3400-1 Story Elements for Middle School Students

Answer Key

1. g. A woodcutter lived on the edge of a forest with his wife and two children.
2. given
3. b. The family was very poor and had no food.
4. l. The mother suggested they lose the children in the forest and let them die there.
5. j. Against his better judgment, the woodcutter very reluctantly agreed.
6. given
7. a. The cottage was made of gingerbread, and the hungry children began to eat it.
8. c. Suddenly an old woman appeared at the door and invited them in for a meal.
9. i. Soon the children realized she was really a wicked witch who planned to eat them.
10. given
11. f. One day Gretel tricked the witch and pushed her into the hot oven.
12. k. Next, Gretel freed her brother from the stable.
13. given
14. h. The children found their way home at last.
15. given
16. d. The woodcutter was delighted to see his children again.
17. given
18. e. And they lived happily ever after. Sentence 11 is the climax.

Proverbs . . . . pp. 36–37
1. g
2. d
3. c
4. f
5. Answers will vary. Students' synopses should be based on proverb a, b, or e.

Spin Action . . . . p. 38
1. 3, 1, 2
2. 1, 2, 3
3. 2, 1, 3
4. 2, 3, 1
5. 2, 1, 3
6. 2, 3, 1

Which Person? . . . . p. 39
1. 2
2. 1
3. 3
4. 1
5. 2
6. 3
7. 3
8. 2
9. 2
10. 1

Neutral News Clips? . . . . p. 40
1. b, the need for improved snow removal equipment; more money should be available
2. a
3. b, sloppily written signs; Understandably the demonstrators drew jeers; much-needed jobs
4. c, only 425 fans; is further indication of the public's lack of interest; Perhaps if more adults in the community supported

Your Analysis . . . . p. 41
1. Tiffany was curious, easily bored, and perhaps not too careful.
2. an old shed in her grandmother's backyard
3. Tiffany needs help; she can't get up after falling.
4. Perciville was the head of the pirates, he was "gentlemanly." James was a mean pirate, unconcerned about scaring women and children.
5. Perciville wanted James to be a more honorable and dignified pirate.
6. Perciville might have a frank discussion with James, or he might ask James to leave the ship.
7. Ryan is a bossy older brother who is mean to his younger brother. Cody is tolerant of some bad behavior but has his limits.
8. the living room
9. Cody wants Ryan to change his behavior.

Misfits . . . . pp. 42-43
1. In horse-and-buggy days, farmers did not use machines to milk. Wooden buggy wheels were more likely than metal ones. Because of the difficulty of the trip to the farm, it is unlikely the doctor would give up so quickly and go home before the baby was born. If it was to be a difficult birth, as a doctor he likely would want to be there. Also, it's unlikely there were phones on which Landis could call.
2. First, Tom is sitting in the lunchroom; then suddenly he's in a classroom.
3. If Mr. Clancy's mind is really "sharp as a tack," he wouldn't have made a mistake with Jonathan's change. Jonathan's purchase was only 15 cents, so he should have received 10 cents, not 5 cents, in change. Also, it is doubtful that a candy shop would sell lawn and garden tools.
4. A digital watch with an alarm would not have been in use at the same time newspapers were typeset with inked letters. Also, it's hard to believe that someone so accustomed to working with deadlines would fail to meet his cousin at the train station. Even more unbelievable is the fact that he was often unreliable, as implied by his last statement.

Diagnosis . . . . p. 45
1. by her children's lives
2. MS causes her to be tired, keeps her from doing a lot of things she wants to do, and prevents her from going out in the sun; sometimes she limps or needs a wheelchair.
3. No information is included about a location. It is set in the present day.
4. perhaps to let others know that a chronic illness does not have to ruin a person's life; to encourage others who face obstacles
5. Those were not the purposes for which the author wrote the story.
6. Before: age 31; married with two young children; did bookkeeping, volunteer work, yard work, canning, and sewing; was content
   After: age 45; married with two teenagers; still parents her kids; learns about her disease; usually feels content
7. perhaps a feeling of hopelessness and helplessness, like an overwhelming obstacle was blocking her path for her life; she calls it the wall of the fear of the unknown.
8. brick by brick, meaning that one day at a time or one small accomplishment at a time she broke down the barrier; it may have also been demolished by learning about her disease and how to treat it
9. At the end of the article, the author says she is content—usually.

48

0-7696-3400-1 *Story Elements for Middle School Students*